Never Outgrow Small Boreens

Martine O'Donovan

This book is dedicated to John Hannigan, an inspiration.

Acknowledgement

Heartfelt thanks to my family and friends for their support and to Orla Kelly for helping me to bring this book to life.

"We have two lives, and the second one begins when we realise we only have one".
- Confucius

Contents

Introduction

This book is an exploration of some of life's experiences. Touching on crushing bewildering losses during childhood and adulthood, the powerful love of family and friends. Balancing them with the steadfast healing found in nature. The utter resilience of the human spirit and the joy of being alive and to experience it to the fullest.

The elemental beauty of the County Waterford coastline is a constant source of wonder as I witness nature going through her rhythms. Our creative souls relish time spent on these activities. It brings peace and contentment and extraordinary healing.

Life takes us down all types of paths. My hope is that we never tire of new adventures best found on small remote roads.

It is hope that propels us forward.
Martine

A Moment of Meditation

Wings carry me across cliffs and coves
Skimming swiftly silently
over clear calm waters
My form reflected
taken by unseen hands
across the bay

Fish teeming below
Eyed by gulls above
The magnetic pull of souls
Immersed in Atlantis
A joyful reminder of the
coats of flesh they wear
I cast my eye on Brownstown
where my form is gently placed
amongst grasses, sand and sea pinks

Winter, Tramore Bay

12 and ¾

Lissom limbed, leaning forward
frown of concentration
upon the smooth forehead
Gentle fingers cheek tapping
immersed in Lord of the Rings
Dark head upon translucent skin
My young boy-man
the eve of his thirteenth year
Muscle chasing bone
Voracious limbs spreading
Restless foot tapping
Proud owner of size seven feet
Pointing to them he asks
When did that happen?
In moments of sleep
The young child's face remains
but less so now
Emerging angular jaw
and sleeping form
filling his bed space
How did I miss that?
Eagle-eyed, maternal
that surreptitious leap
taken in darkness
Was my back turned?
But for a moment

Aftermath

He was contrite in that moment
Well, he believed he was anyway

I, on the other hand didn't fall for it

Patterns played out, old and familiar

As sure as stones drop into the lake
Ever decreasing circles form and

merge into the grasses at its edge
As sure as night follows day

He will be contrite again

Autumn

Soft freckled faces and sunkissed skin
Consigned to scratchy grey trousers
Tightly laced shoes and choking shirts
Constricting movements brings
Summers' freedoms to a close
Cooler sharp mornings
followed by glorious midday sun
Hurrying home to catch its last
before dusk draws its fragrant curtain
Early fires settle into
a gentle grey billowing
Equinox is upon us
the drawing in to ourselves
for times of quiet reflection
In the embers of Autumn fires

Blue

I am sky on sunshine filled days
Cool and dusky at twilight
I am night sky sprinkled with light
from lifetimes ago
I search between the stars for answers
I am reflected on lakes on clear mornings
Dragonflies skim above unbroken membranes
I am Archangels' cloak of protection
I am sky white seagull pierces
Brilliant scavenger never hungers
I am blue rocks the salty foam engulfs
I am blue spark that ignites life
flickers crystalises creates worlds
I am avenue of expression
from which blue words come
I am black blue Raven
piercing hearts with black thoughts
I am blue sun filled ocean
As By The Sea Sailors
cast their gelatinous sails
Trusting the winds
I am blue veins
carrying blood to each cell
The ultimate connection
The Pia Mater
Faithful mother
Cloaked in Blue

Broken

It was the last vestige of things precious
that brought my mother to her knees

The large water filled globe containing
Our Lady of Lourdes
had been knocked to the floor through
childish horseplay

She knelt in front of the t.v.
in a pool of shattered glass and plastic flowers
Her tears falling into the puddle

She looked broken
Like one of those donkeys you see on television
ruined and beyond repair
The last momento from her mother's house

I didn't understand the levels of her loss then
What this represented in her shattered life
as a battered wife
There was no more

She whimpered as she knelt
and plucked the shards from the floor
from her bloody nylons
Her silent tears more fearful than her rant

Brother Love

I lay my head on shore pebble beds
and drew down the plough
with the pads of my fingers
They poked the moon to life
I kicked it into touch and
watched it melt on the horizon
I asked them could I stay
as you lay in the cold drawer allotted you
Me, feeling your aloneness
that you could no longer
and wondered how I would
go on without you

Chain Reaction

My mother opened the latch on the gate without getting off her bike. She glided down my grandmother's yard, crossing her leg gracefully through the middle and coming to a stop next to the pansies under the windowsill. Her drindl skirt flared out from her tiny belted waist. Her cardigan, open and pushed up sleeves revealed freckled forearms. Her glorious mane of red hair held in check with a white hairband. Her chocolate brown eyes shone. My four-year-old self did not realise that my mother was then only twenty-six, but I knew she was beautiful. The sun seemed to shine for her. She turned to play with the chain on the bike. Moments later, my mother cried out in pain. The chain had snapped back into place snagging one of her fingers on the metal teeth and held it in its iron grip.

"Mammy!" she cried out. She sounded like a child. She cried like a child. When I saw her finger impaled with blood flowing freely, I instantly felt her pain in my finger. I had to bite mine to relieve the sensation as my grandmother rushed out to her and tended to the gaping wound.

It was my earliest realisation that my mother wasn't invincible, and even on beautiful sunny days, bad things can happen.

Christmas Eve

A time honoured promise
Not to make any purchases today
Fire burning brightly since dawn
A cocoon of food preparation
Listening to Christmas in Vienna
as I peel and chop and stir
Soft lights twinkle dull December light
The nourishment of a loved house
reminds me of my blessings

I recall with a smile
the open mouth of my Ex as I cry
"No!", an untamed shrew
as he tipped the pot of cooling stock
down the sink in an attempt to help
Grounds for divorce in itself
I wasn't smiling then

The candle on the table
burns brightly for those loved
lost and yearned for
My heart and eyes full
when I think of them

I recall my mother and I
sitting together, pulling bread apart
and eye-watering onions chopped
for stuffing in the white Pyrex bowl
The two chickens stuffed to feed us ten

Answering the discreet knock
at nightfall in my eleventh year
Receiving the cardboard box
from the local charity
My utter despondence discovering
there was no Santa
I went through the stranger's gifts
wrapping them for the little ones
asleep upstairs
I crept into bed that night and cried

Being sent into town in darkness
My sister and I
Searching the noisy pubs
for our father in shadowy corners
Pleading mother's words to come home
with some of his wage
Fearfully reading his expression
When glassy eyes look our way
Fish out of water
Childhood gone now
Like cold ashes left in the morning grate

My own children's faces
Come into view
Eyes shining in anticipation
Tucked up with their teddies
Sleep defying them
The leap of the generations
Gratifyingly Profound

Colm's Jumper

I wore it for three months
until I could smell him no longer
The black fisherman's jumper
thick cable stitch
Died in his bed over granny's head
Sleeves are unravelling
I tuck it under my wrist
 play with the knots I've created
She thought he was snoring
It was choking she heard
His blonde hairs are interwoven
with the wool in places
He is still with me in part
Granny gave him mouth to mouth
when he was four hours dead
Her futile love breath
could not penetrate
the place he now dwelt
The aroma of his skin
rose up to me
from the hot wool at night
the taste of vomit
filled my mouth
as I slept in the single bed
with my grandmother
Both eking comfort
from each others' warmth
as we listened to
our startled breaths

Curled up and Cornered

Your hatred of me was beyond my understanding
The blackened eyes looked
as if their soul had retreated
to a sanctuary
somewhere outside of you
What remained was wounded and snarling
Curled up and cornered
Ready to attack
Teeth bared and mouth foaming
Unreachable
Pleasured only by inflicting pain
Your hatred of you was beyond my understanding
On your deathbed
The sacred light of love and grace
filled your eyes and softened your face
As I read from your prayer book
"I'm fucked, aren't I?"
You held my gaze
Knowing I wouldn't lie
You closed your eyes and found the peace
you couldn't while alive

Dangerous Waters

It was twenty dusty steps
with a turn half way
Like the landing on the stairs
as we took the steps
by the school bridge
down to the river

Dandelions and buttercups
littered the corners
in gay confusion
amongst empty crisp packets
and cigarette butts
left by older students

Brambles and nettles
covered the wall
as you approached the
quickening river

Can I draw your picture
and i'll give you some sweets?
Young and curious
but clever enough to see
the darkness that hung around him
We turned and took the steps
back up in breathless twos

Daughter Dear

I gaze upon your sleeping form
curled up with your teddy
It's hard to tell where it ends
and you begin
Your hair of glory curls
round the nape of your neck
Eyelids flutter softly in dreams

Your entrance into the world was hard
It left its mark
My dreams for you daughter
are filled with hope and love
and the fierceness of wants
for your steadfast happiness
when challenges come your way
The ache of you floods my heart
I slip the soother from your lips
and leave it just within your reach

Day at the Races

"If I catch ye, I'll make bloody mincemeat out of ye!" raged one of the mothers raising her sweeping brush over her head in an attempt to frighten us. Proper little brats were we, not a care in the world when it came to their flowers. During the summer holidays, we would organise horse racing competitions, ourselves being both jockey and horse. Who would be placed first, second and third, and on the following days trying to maintain or better your position having an overall winner by the end of the week. The glory of being the fastest on the street. By the time you would be finished, it was hard to decide what was the sorest, your hands or your arse.

Our homes were tiny two up, two down, housing far more than the prescribed rooms. No form of heating apart from the open fire in the kitchen. Going to bed cold and getting up cold was an everyday occurrence apart from the spectacular Summer holidays when our world became lovely. The houses sat on a very steep hill with small front gardens ringed with concrete walls. Eleven gardens in total on the hill, with a bend towards the bottom creating a potential bottleneck for the jockeys.

The height difference between one garden and another made the jumps more challenging. Sometimes landing in the lower garden at high speed resulted in falling and tumbling bodies landing on you before you could get up and keep running. Most of the gardens were well maintained with shrubs and flowers. To see fifteen children standing on the top wall brought an excitement to your chest that was hard to put into words. Standing stock still. All of the smaller children who couldn't climb the walls yet, looking up in admiration, awaiting "On yer marks. Get set. Go!!"

The palpable roar as thirty legs thrummed across the grass in a stampede, the height differential being reasonably equal for the first three walls. As the steep incline approached, the walls went from thigh level on one side to above your head on the other side. Some opting to hang over the wall and drop to their feet, not brave enough to jump. This created further mayhem with experienced jumpers landing on hangers-on and Trixie the dog delirious with so many legs in his garden running left and right his small body jumping out of its skin to attack.

The final leg of three tiny gardens on the bend took out some of the less experienced in the crush and tumble. Hearts pumping in sweaty bodies carrying trophies of cut legs, cut elbows, scratched faces, trampled gardens and angry mothers. Oh the joys of winning in the melee, and to get to do it all again tomorrow.

Delectable Dereliction

The cottage roof
 a ramshackled assortment of gaps
like the smiling face of a first communion child
Smoke once belched from the chimney
to the rhythms of the household
Whitewashed walls crumbling
the ivy marching forward
Its silent army maintaining its stay

The front door a barrier to that inner sanctuary
Permission granted to the souls who knocked
to cross the threshold
Blistered paint now dancing on loose hinges
Decades of weather endured
A testimony to its worn armour

Souls no longer knock
at the door where no one lives
But life still ambles on
Chicks cry from chimney pots
demanding to be fed
The rust encrusted gate
covered in a profusion of roses
Blushed cheeks raised to the sky
Dandelions and daisies sway
Tempting butterflies and bees to stay
and bask in the glory of its remoteness

Days of Wonder

In shady spots, dewdrops hold on
steadfastly in the knowledge
their battle will be lost by noon
Tantalising breezes warm
sea grasses
Like waves upon water
Their synchronised dance
choreographed by the moon

Dusty buttercups edge the cliffs
A million small suns
face the blue blue sky
Seagull charts my course
On sacred airbuilt thoroughfares
Come Holy Spirit Guide
I hear myself say
Wishing I had wings
as he soars Heavenward

Dog Days

I gripped my mother's hand
helping her over the stile
Her balance off kilter
in advancing pregnancy
The short cut through the fields
saved the long walk to the hospital

The previous days rains
created a treacherous path
as we carefully picked our muddy steps

In the gap of the approaching field
two heads appeared
Guard dogs from the neighbouring house
loose and approaching
Slow menacing feet bared teeth
Hypnotic as they inched forward

A silent trigger launched
a mauling sprint
Their movements mirrored
Giant Alsatian heads
locked in murderous glint
rising into the air

One fluid single whistle
Mingled with our screams
In perfect symmetry
both dogs stopped at our feet
turned and walked away
I have no doubt there was
Divine Intervention that day

Drawing from the Well

I place my hands upon its stony surface
and stare into its blank darkness
The work reaps cool water
for our hot throats
our parched souls
Gifts of suffering rarely seen
for the jewels that they are
These are the best of times
The all to do turmoil
of normal happiness
Of just being alive

St Patrick's Well, Clonmel, Co Tipperary

Equinox

It rained all day
my treacherous soul
knee deep in its obfuscate reckonings
Autumnal rains lashed my brow
small horsewhip cracks
Chance offerings to trounce me ever down
or beat me into a new shape
Bilious moon bid me an implacable nod
Its green gaze drank in
what little light there was
Til morning shook its sleepy head
and poured its delight over
all of the dark places

Estuary Reflections

Golden grasses sway on summer's breath
exhaled gently by Mother Nature
in her lush sensual movements
Dust pockets spring from hidden places
beneath the golden gorse
Skylark's ascent
her song filling blue blue skies

The air, heady with its sweet scent
mingled with salty seaweed
drying in the sunshine

Estuary birds preening feeding
enjoying days of abundance
Interlacing patterns from tiny webbed feet
a Greek papyrus scroll
lying undiscovered on warm sand
until ebbing tide returns to claim it
erasing it from memory

Occasional poppies, their faces
opening in delight
Cabbage Whites place their feet
softer than baby's breath upon sea pinks
Such tiny hearts lift gentle wings to flight

The warmth of the day gives way
to crackling campfire
against the jet black sky
The cape of the Toreador upon the water
Moon draws her skirts up to full height
lighting up the night sky
Curlews hearld her arrival

She is my touch,my sights, my sounds
She is my breath, She is breathtaking
I am all that is Nature
Nature is all that I am

Everheart

As my remains
Lie in their silk lined box
Hands crossed over my heart
Enveloped in a cloak of darkness
beneath the soil

My face,
Stripped clean by mother nature
The essence of who I was
shapeshifted like windblown sand
Remembered by few
A return to white
A return to the light

Life's breath long gone
Taking with it
Fears, criticisms, guilt
The rat-race, the grieving, the pain

Corporeal chains released
space filled with nothingness
but peace, perfect peace

Gentle eyes, through which expressions
of love were mirrored
now hollowed and bare

Gentle hands, my greatest gift of all
for fulfilling my soul's desires
My loving companions
still now, and
placed upon the sweet silent heart

Gentle feet, I have looked down upon you
from first tentative steps
You led me down life's paths
together we stood at crossroads
my willing companions
now carelessly crumbling
In a state of grace

My heartfelt thanks
I offer you, my humble abode
for time spent in each other's company
You have served me well
Death, my friend
pays tribute to my life's work
with the gift of everlasting peace

First Mothering

It took three months
for the first utterance
to slip from her lips
She let her guard down
for just a moment
The smiling nun's skirts
swished softly on
polished herringbone floors
handed her a brush
and some paints
Carefully taped
some paper to the desk
and gently said
You can paint
anything you want

Glendalough

Ancient burial grounds
Invite all who tread there
to experience its' quiet majesty
A verdant cloak envelops you
Gently reminding
how small we are in this world
and our troubles too

The old tree stands quietly
resting by the sparkling stream
Watery sounds fill my ears
as it winds its way over stones
glistening in the sunlight

I inhale the damp mossy earth
that had settled itself around its base
Reaching out to touch its softness
A peace, deep and ancient settles over me

God Willing

The mossy fabric stitched together
by the most patient of hands
beckons me to rest
Here I can scrape away
the rabid attention
thoughts give my old shattered self

Placing my hands upon your trunk
I ask that you imbue me with strength
You gently sway when resistance is futile
Suggesting I must do the same

Generously patterned earthy gauze
Roots run deep and wide
connecting to elemental magic
in your loamy depths

A lifetime of standing
Your strength and grace
is painfully inched out
Bearing witness to storms
Gathering patience for sunshine
To pour magic upon your being and mine

Gods and Ghouls

Grandad's long period of vacant spells lapsed into a full stroke. I watched in mute disbelief from the end of his single bed as Granny and her neighbour propped him up on a mountain of pillows. His eye and jaw hung like a broken gate as they tried to get some water into his unresponsive mouth. They looked like two flapping hens from the yard below. Their large bums wrapped in their navy floral bibs as they swiftly moved to make him comfortable.

My grandmother's hands would absently pat the front pockets of her apron throughout the day as if trying to recall where she had left something down. Rubbing her large floury palms on her hips as she worked the silken dough at the kitchen table making bread for the nuns. She would give me a small piece to play with. Later on, she would put it in the oven for me, and I'd devour it with her homemade strawberry jam.

"No! He will choke on the water, he has lost his swallow."
"Can you go and get the Doctor ? "
"Love, I think we should call for an ambulance."

The gentle man loved his pipe after his day's work and an occasional Guinness. The bottle was carefully placed on the red lino next to his work boots. His workhorse hands would cup the walnut base of his pipe. Inspecting the ingrained oil under his fingernails and painted on his flesh bones, I thought about the kind of work he did. I'd seen him rise from his pew mid-Mass when the siren rang calling for firemen. Retired almost a year, I liked to read the inscription on the fancy clock on the mantelpiece that they gave him.

Sitting next to him, I'd watch him clean and refill his pipe. Softly tapping the chamber to loosen the spent leaves and packing it with fresh ones. The delicious smell of sulphur from the stricken match; the hot hollow sound of the suck as he placed the bit in his mouth. Hair oil from his head on the inside of his peaked cap upon his knee. The cream diamond shape of silk material with a small red stitch keeping it in place. The maker's name in writing in the centre, lying on top of his head each day. I picked it up and buried my face in it. His scent laid down in my memory. The small houndstooth pattern felt hairy under my fingertips. I lay my head against his arm, his shirt smelling of tar and sweet sweat. I inhaled his smoke in blissful silence.

When I was younger and fanciful in my imagination, I found fearful places all over the house. The cubby hole behind the sofa in the sitting room had a small door that restrained my downstairs monsters. Mercifully, it was rarely opened except by my grandad who kept all manner of things in there like chimney brushes and work things. I remained well back on the occasions when the chair was pulled out from the wall.

The weather dial in the tiny hall held me in utter fascination as I spied "Fair" on its polished face. I regularly opened the front door to check if the weather outside matched it, transfixed by its magic. The climb up the narrow, steep stairs was shrouded in dread as I approached the holy water font on the landing made from seashells. I ducked under it so as not to be seen passing. The blanket box my father had made was placed in the front bedroom under the eaves. It contained most of the upstairs monsters with the exception of those held captive within the patterns on the large wardrobe. I spied my terrified face reflected in its rigorously polished surface. The shadow shapes holding me captive in their gaze.

I look at the holy picture above my head from my single bed. My position, mimicking the pose of Jesus Christ, His heart exposed in sepia tones. Eyes lifted towards heaven in supplication, the crown of thorns embedded into His skull. I inspect each thorn set deep in flesh, grotesque in their size. His mortal blood flowing from each impalement and spilling down His neck. My eyes trace their course towards His open heart with the love light surrounding it. His gentle wounded hands raised either side. An open gesture of love.

As I looked up, the top of my head touched the base of the heavily pointed frame. I pushed against it and feeling a little pain I tried to imagine His. How could He help me from within the confines of the glass if the shadow monsters on the wardrobe door awoke? I held an infirm belief that if the enormous frame didn't fall and kill me while I slept, it would protect me from the evil residing within the wardrobe. I pulled the heavily starched linen up under my chin and prayed until sleep laid its fragrant mantle over me.

Grandad now lies in this bed. With all of the might of an eleven-year old, I gaze at the Sacred Heart and plead silent prayers to spare him.

"Let's get you off to school now, there's a good girl."

"What? Can I not stay?"

"You will be better off in school."

Grandad died a week later. I buried my face in his cap and cried.

He came to me in my dreams last night. I stood in Leukman's old Chemist shop. Wooden floors, shelves and apothecary drawers, complete with a cash register with the pointing finger. A sanitized smell hung in the air. He walked over to me and smiled. I spoke, and tears ran freely. I was conscious enough within the dream to be aware that it was one. It has been forty years since he had walked in my dreams. The man who taught me how to proudly light a fire without a firelighter. Together we would sit looking into the flames. Him puffing on his pipe and me basking in his gentle company.

Heartspace

Dancing to its own tune
I inhale and quietly listen
for the infinitesimal pause
between lub and dup
The rise and fall
Dusk and Dawn
Sun and Moon
Its precious momentum
Sees me through each moment
While it laughs, or
picks up the broken pieces
and puts me together again
For anger or passionate love
For blood spilled in war
Brings a hardening
A tightening of vessels
For emerging new souls
washed clean at birth
with their mother's love
placed upon the breast
what lies beneath
that familiar beat
heard from the womb
Bringing expansion
It all comes from the heart
and through it
Give thanks
to that precious place
Acknowledge and love
Your Heartspace

His Brown Shoes

Along the harbour road in Baltimore among
the clanging of boats and seagulls cries
I saw you lying there and with a slow heave
I sat you upon the low wall

You were waiting for the bus
Your wife was unwell
You had to get home
Again you fell, harder this time
Your net bag carrying your milk and bread
created a glassy stream towards the pier

You spoke through bloodied teeth
Gripping my hand
She will be waiting
I placed my coat beneath your head
Help is on the way I said

It was then I saw your brown shoes
The same shoes sat beneath
my father's hospital bed
I used to look at them next to the urine bag
and wonder would you put your feet
into them again

They were bundled into a blue sack
the day you died and returned to our mother
The moment wrapped me in hollow regret

Sandhills from the Saleens

I can almost see the sea!

Tumbling into the car
the space between us
Gone with all of our yesterdays
Grubby knees in hot huddles
Buckets under our feet
Sticky fingers hold lollipops
that burn the insides of our cheeks

A promise of icecreams on the way home
The crunch of wafer and flake
There it is! I can see the sea

We run like warriors into battle
towards sparkling waters
Throwing caution to the wind
our sandals and socks
Greeting it like a long lost friend
who has waited for our return

Sandcastles, rock forts and moats
Feathers and shells for little boats
Daddy gets chips and lemonade
Bellys' full we lie in shade
We watch gulls cry as they land
swoop and pierce the sky

Now our tumble is not so frantic
as we pack into the car
Tired, hot and happy
Sand sand everywhere

We wait outside the shop for cones
I can almost see the sea
receding in the rear car window
as we make our journey home

I was looking for something that wasn't there

I was looking for something that wasn't there
in the faces of others
Their opinions of me mattered more than I care
The half experiences in handing over
the seat of my power
Dragged through life on whims of others
Creates a tiredness hard to define
It's time to claim what's rightfully mine
The soul's remarkably forgiving you see
All I was looking for is inside of me

In Memory of My Mother

My mother paved the way for me
What attributes of hers do I see?
I hear her laugh in mine as clear as a bell
and
an occasional glance
Is more hers as well

I look at my hands, and as they grow older
It's hers I see, looking back at me

She did not protect me from violence
For she was incapable of protecting herself
Each blow softened her light
to a dull intractable glow

My mother paved the way for me
It will take a lifetime to understand
gifts when wrapped in doubt
My turn has come
to dig to sow and reap, and
Characteristics of my own to keep

My daughter will have her moments too
When traits will mirror her mother
The passage of time not hers, not mine
Trades gifts with one another

It's now or never

Gertrude Brennan was an ordinary woman. Her characterless quality imbued a sense of the invisible. Walking along the street that bleak morning, she stared at her image in the shop window. In the weak morning light, her scraped back brown hair, and intense brown eyes betrayed her inner wretchedness. She walked up the side street and unlocked the doors to Murphy's Undertakers, where she worked as an Embalmer.

The fluorescent light hummed yellow as it warmed up, giving the room a bare bone feeling. Gertrude worked mostly alone. John Junior had arrived back from the states six months earlier. Broke his mother's heart with assault charges. He had a way about him. Gertrude fell hard for his charms. "We'll go away tonight, I promise. Just this one more job eh?"

Working with the fluids of the dead, she rolled out the 70-year-old and commenced his arterial embalming. She finally placed the bag of diamonds in his throat as Johnny had instructed. His contact would retrieve them that night before the grave was filled in. Johnny would collect her at 10 pm, and they would leave this town for good.

She sat in her sitting room that night and listened to the weighted ticking of the clock, her brown suitcase by her feet. The silent room filled with the congestion of her thoughts. He didn't come. What was she thinking? She put her coat on at 11.30 pm, walked out into the soft drizzle and down the dark lane towards the cemetery until she found the grave. Her brown shoes sinking in the freshly turned clay, the heavy drizzle sticking. Murderous thoughts rose within her. What a foolish woman she was. She would kill him for this.

Hearing movement behind her, she turned and faced the spade Johnny brought with force down on her forehead. He removed the green matting and tumbled dead Gertrude into the open grave. Her unseeing eyes never felt the clay enter them. Johnny shovelled soil until Gertrude was no more. Replacing the planks, he walked on through the dead without a backwards glance.

Journey

I stare at

my own diminishing substance

Leaching in rivulets towards the handbasin

I do not recognise the wailing soul

and the levels of her pain

It abates

Relief floods in

Tho' treachery lies in its abeyance

for all the while it is gathering

for a resurgence

The guiles of the soul are many

as this unseasoned usurper

charts her course

Tree in Acrylics, Glendalough, Co Wicklow

June

I wandered into woodlands
In June rain after drought
The taste of clay, it's turfy tang
hung rich inside my mouth
Green sap on blackened bark
droplets settle on my face
Steaming cattle in bleeding streams
Its beauty leaves its trace

A field of crows pulled fattened worms
gorge on their grassy feast
The wild Woodbine on hedgerows
makes sweet the air for birds and beast
Scudding clouds go tumbling fast
as grey skies clear to blue
Sunshine filled the pastures
with greens and golds of every hue

On fireside days when wont to gaze
I think of warmer times
When cattle crunch on Summer grass
and swish their tails at errant flies
It leaves my mind to wander
down lanes of linen and lace
With sweeping smile I stay awhile
In pastures green, my sacred place

Love Well Placed

It was incumbent upon me to do something in that moment
A gesture, however small
I placed my hands upon her frail shoulders
Her broken heart, witnessed
He made short work of death
For that at least she was grateful
Her heart spilled open
The healing had started

Mammy Goes Commando

The day dawned like any other in some respects. A cold bright February day with steely sunshine and wind that would cut you in two. A time of rebirth and renewal. Plants continued to push their delicate young heads from under the cold hard soil towards the light after their dormancy. The morning birds rose from their beds and danced in the morning skies. Each family member woke with their own feeling of something hard and indigestible in the pits of their stomachs. A taste of shock on the tongue robbing it of all of its usual wants. A dreadful dawning. Their son and youngest brother had taken his life. His body lay in the mortuary. They were waiting for him to come home.

The apple of his mother's eye. Gentle creature, struggling with dark days and a battle to continue walking through life's journey. The skin stripped from their bones and exposed to that icy February wind left them raw and hollowed to the core. Mouths left half-open with questions that robbed them of their sleep. Fruitless questions cried out alone. A pain in the heart space that could not be softened. No amount of hugs or soft words would immolate the feeling that poured itself into a series of endless black shapes.

What is the parting gift of the dead? Is it being shook to the core brings a realisation that we really do love each other? Can we use these experiences to recalibrate our own hearts and heal old wounds?

The remaining family members huddled together around the kitchen table. One could cut a swathe through the smoke-filled room. The table heaved with endless rounds of untouched cakes and sandwiches.

Old photographs were pulled out and passed around. A reminder of how beautiful he was. How precious. Stories shared where one would start, and another would finish. Other extracts added that were not known by some brought smiles. The tapestry of this young man's life woven tightly by family; intricate and brightly coloured, ensuring their memories were kept alive. That he was kept alive. There would be an autopsy. It would be a further six months before there was a verdict from the Coroner. Another sentence.

"Anyone else for tea?"
"Your mother will probably have some," Dad said.

Mammy crossed the kitchen returning to the armchair. Gentle and ladylike in her ways, and well practised in the art of silent disapproval. Our loss so great, but incalculable for the one who carried him in her belly.

"I don't think I should. I'm on my water tablets at the moment".
"A small cup of tea won't do any harm Mam".
 "I'm having trouble with my waterworks. I was already down to my last piece of underwear ".

"Do you mean to say that you are sitting there with no knickers on?"

"No, I've none on," she replied, eyes downcast, hands folded in her lap.
She raised her countenance higher in the chair in dignified silence.

"Well, I never thought I'd see the day that I could say Mammy goes Commando",
 "and you wonder why there are eight of us ?" one of the girls said, turning to her father.

Stunned silence was followed by an outpouring of hysterical laughter which they drank deeply from. Happy tears flowed freely as the spirit of their loved one laughed with them. They would survive this.

Maps

There is an unfurling of tracks
highways and byways
Laid down through
generations of footfall
Striations traversed
by animal man and machine
Places to come, to go
Places to live and die

I feel the foliage beneath my feet
 the dampness, the coolness
 I inhale the pine needles
a verdant carpet upon the forest floor
I watch insect life upon tree bark
 Ants, fervent in the care of their Queen
 Observing the tipping point
 ensuring the balance is struck

Mating calls and ravenous chicks
fed by exhausted parents
darting about catching breakfast
upon the wing
Watery sounds of silver streams
Mossy stones carpeting
the bed of a watery world
illuminating sunlight on
gently rustling leaves

I look to these reference points
for the journey within
It will yield a world of treasures
not found on any map

Moonlit Cliff Walk (on the lovely Doneraile)

Ground crisp as the bite from an apple
crunched cleanly underfoot
Tentative steps taken in places
where moonlight failed to reach
cast its' silver cloak across the water
reaching to where I stood
All seeing eyes in the darkness
Twinkling lights upon the water
Men cast their nets and waited

Gentle hush of the waves
lapping at the cliff face
like a mother's hand
caressing her child's head
Flickering flashes
weaving on the crest of waves

meeting moonbeams
butterfly kisses on cool skin
Not day, not night, this dazzling light
as it weaves its magic
A silver world; grass fence cove
melted by the artist's glaze

Mrs McKenna's Ham

"Why did Willy have to sell the shop?" Mary asked her aunt while she carefully set the fire the way her grandfather taught her. She lit the match and watched the flame as it curled its way round the paper and licked the sticks. A yellow flame, not yet warmed. An adult task for her proud ten years.

"Poor Willy's health hasn't been the best, and His Lordship will be home soon. Pop down to Willy's and get me some ham for this salad."

"How can we keep calling the shop Willy's, Aunty Marley?"
"It won't matter whose name is over the bloody door, so long as we can still get our groceries. I don't fancy the cycle to town."

"Get me eight slices."
Mrs McKenna put her children in the shop window to play. Both were filthy. Opening the shop door, Mary could smell a dirty nappy.

"What can I get you love?"
"Can I have eight slices of ham please?"

She cut the ham on the slicer, placing a sheet of paper to catch the curling slivers. A very small boy walked over to his mother, snivelling. His snotty nose resembled two church candles. Mrs McKenna, took the snot between her fingers from the boy's nose and rubbed it on the side of her apron. She then picked up the ham with the snotty fingers and placed the meat in the bag. Mary handed over the fiver, took her change and ran from the shop.

In gasps, she retold the story to her aunt. Mary didn't know what mystified her more; the snot incident, or her aunt's laughter.

"Let's just give His Lordship the ham, and don't breathe a word !"

"I think I'll just have the bread.." replied Mary.

My Grandmother

I wrote letters to her every week
for six months
No response ever came
from the iron lung she lay in
How can you be in one
when lungs are on the inside?
The pain felt
could not be reached by any hand
When they put her in the ground
I could not go
I dug my nails into the earth on
the ice cold potatoes
under winter tap water
Small emolliation
for my broken heart
Stinging tears striking cold fingers
On the cusp of teenage years
Utterly lost without her

Nan 96

Taken
From her dwelling place
To her final resting place
A life long and fruitful
Four score and many more
A century minus four
Creeping forward from birth
With youth beauty and grace
Smiling eyes delightful face
Orphaned in childhood
Missed her porridge
More than her mammy
Belly rumbling
Walking barefoot to school
Experienced love loss and pain
Like the fleeting seasons
Ever moving forward
Don't look back
A long life? Not long enough?
Not the time spent here
But how

October Treasures

Snarling winds snatch'd breath from my open mouth
Whip crack'd hair lashes my stinging face
God's angry stirring creates thunderous roilling
of limpid waters
that creates an aliveness within

Estuary birds remain hidden
while seagull attempts jerky airstreams
Forges ahead
watching the kite surfer below him
Harnessing the wind
Striking a glancing blow
Devouring argumentative waters
Red sail slashing grey skies

October is leaving us
It is the way of things
The intemperance of these days
are gathering momentum

An Sean Phobail (Old Parish)

The rocks proudly display mossy coats
to all who pass their way
while covetous ivy insinuates
in quiet encroachment
Paired to the bone shrubs shiver and dance
to the tune playing in the bay
Gulls on the breeze
piercing sky like silver arrows
I taste the clay of the ploughed fields in my mouth
scraping the butter on my potato

Rooks cascade and settle
on the sunshine warmed green barn
Their joyful murmuration
each turn of wing an invitation
The blue stone waters remain tranquil
despite the off shore winds
As all movement is held under
the solid gaze of the lighthouse

Rest

Let the silken silence settle
On your prostrate form
Veil of blue
Banket of green
Earth and Sky
Their protective presence
Balancing notes
Orchestral sounds
Of sacred fluids
Ebb and flow
Our faithful mother within

She whispers to you;
In times of turbulence
She gently draws you in
Calls you home
To yourself
Offering the gift
of dying a little daily
The sleep of a child
In silken silence
muddied waters settle
and healing begins

Revelations

She likened me to
riding a mechanical horse
wielding a sword
Slashing clouds of heaven
into tiny white slivers
Fastidious in my care
to repair
such insuperable tasks
unwanted and unresolved
A battle among giants
witnessed from a safe harbour
But not safe at all
until i surrender
my swords of doubt
fighting battles
already lost
and won

Sequoia

The very sight of you filled me with awe
My neck ached as I craned skyward
through your branches
They seemed to touch the heavens
It was as though the very earth moved on your breath

I placed my hands
upon your soft pliable skin
You smelled of sweetened turf
It took four of us holding hands
to embrace you fully

The large nails hammered into you
made footholds as we climbed
The notoriety of who was brave
enough to climb highest
and make it safely down

Who planted the Sequoia in
in the grounds of the hospital?
Had he any dreams of
how it might look in maturity?

Stories of near deaths and injury
were polished and handed down
to our younger selves
as our gain and glory was
played out on those days
in the magnificence of your shadow

Seven Deadly Sins

Creeping at dawn into the sleepy silent kitchen, the early summer sun shone through the gold curtains. It filled the ordinary domestic objects with quiet wonder as the drunken particles softly swam. Her nose of four years, level with the kitchen table gazed at the shaft of light, like a spotlight in a circus ring. Not shining on an elephant or tiger but on a bowl of jelly in all of its crimson perfection. A lustrous lake, without a ripple, encased in her grandmother's crystal bowl.

Mouth pooling with saliva, she surreptitiously stuck her small finger into the centre of the irresistible mould. Ensuring just one attempt yielded a bountiful booty; turning her finger towards her and lifting the quivering heap to her lips. Closing her eyes, the morsel melted on her tongue in raspberry rapture.

Mild exhilaration now wrapped in uncertainty, the wet finger pointed accusingly at the gaping hole in the centre of the bowl. That same shaft of sunlight illuminating the wrecked surface.

Thoughts of imminent punishment required a plan of action. Looking around the kitchen, she went to the plastic flower arrangement brought back from Lourdes sitting in the good blue vase. She plucked a flower from it and placed it in the hole in the centre of the jelly. From the kitchen door, she looked back at her handiwork thinking

"Mother will never know".

Shadows

Shadows play upon the wall
on a Summer's evening
lengthened by the setting sun
The Artist's brush held to the canvas
unfolds a series of light and shadow

Calling on our shadow side
calls
courage to the surface
waxing and waning
towards a full moon
time for sleep
rest and recovery
It heralds the morning light
as
shadow follows light
light follows shadow
Played out in this dance
The days of our lives

Sunrise on the Backstrand

The early riser treads the coastal path
Small plumes of dust lifting and
captured in the soft morning light

Skylarks hover on high
Orchestral sounds
heavensent in their sweetness
against the blue blue sky

Soft green grasses sway
As golden sun
Lights up the bay
Basking in gladness

Sleepy souls peep out
to witness its glory
Breathing in the freshness
of early morning air

Swans pass in the gloaming
Dewy white bodies glisten
Their call a prayer

Quivering Curlews
cry from the long grasses
Declaring all is well
As their new day dawns
In the waking bay

Backstrand, Tramore

Skin On, Pin Bones Removed

She had blue skin
and so had I
Her love was mirrored
through feckless eyes
I felt her weight
upon where I lie
She crossed the threshold
of her mortal gate
And left me empty
as hollowed bones
Remorse that I feel
Alas too late

The Angelus from behind the Chair

My grandparents waited for the six o clock gong on TV. Both sat in reverential silence in their patterned floral chairs. I placed my five-year-old hands on the back of my grandmother's chair and watched with quiet fascination her working of the beads through her large hands. It was the one time of the day that my frisky as a lamb self had to be quiet as a mouse or risk the steely gaze of granny.

The fire was laden down with damp slack, and the molten coals beneath worked their way to the surface. The statue of Our Lady by the fireside was bigger than myself, and I coveted the miniature artificial roses in the tiny pot by her feet that fitted snugly into my hand. Their silk petals were unchangeable and lovely. I followed the swirls and whorls on the green carpet to see what corner of the room it would lead me to.

I looked at my grandfather's beautiful, gentle profile as he sat in prayer. He was very quiet these days and spent a lot of time looking into space. I imagined his stubble scratching my chin as he always did, and I felt a giggle leap unannounced from my throat. Granny turned, and the giggle was quickly swallowed. I stared at the picture of the Potato Gatherers; they had also stopped to say their prayers. On the other wall were Pope Paul I and Pope John, The Laughing Pope looking approvingly at the little gathering.

Over my grandmother's shoulder, I spied the china teapot in the glass case that held all of her precious things. There was a Chinese warrior hand-painted on the side of the pot, and I would regularly check that the key in the glass door was locked to ensure that he stayed inside. As I wrestled with the uncertainty of battles with the warrior, the final gong rang, and I could move again.

"Good girl," she said, scooping me up onto her lap and smothering me with kisses. After supper, I'd get a chance to come down and warm myself on the grate before going to bed.

The Hill of the Women

Having a brief moment living in sin
We made our way to the parish hall
for our pre-marriage chat

The priest spoke in parables
The Rhythm Method glossed over
when talk had turned to
How men and women differ

Sex is like climbing a mountain he said
Ye set out together then
Yer man is at the top of Sliabh na Mban
Looking down at you
And you have barely set out on your journey
You call after him
Will you wait for me!

We went home and pulled out
our hiking boots
Just to test his theory

The Junction

Clambering towards
his prone figure
In a fug of fumes
Shadowed fingers claw
and peel back the buckled steel
Traffic light shapeshifting in the evening drizzle
Mouth and nostrils a mass
of shattered glass
Ear torn open like a prayer book

Disconnected sensations
Meld with fragmented sounds
Staring uncomprehendingly
into the paramedics face
He saw the words form
You are lucky to be alive

The Knight of the Sun
Painting by Arthur Hughes c 1860

Devotedly, they carried their Knight
to the closing of the day
His soul preparing its journey
where his broken bones now lay

A Knight noble kind and true
Witnessed golden splendour
bathe his form in the dying light
Birds rejoiced in the thicket
A fanfare befitting
God's soldier returning
to peaceful pastures this night

The Neighbour

She lifted the latch on the back door and let herself in
as she always did
She resembled a line of rusty pump water
The smell of old ash limped around her
as she spoke
Her hair meshed in painful rollers
Haloed in a rat grey netting
Old make-up sat in the hollows of her face
Rivulets in an old well
Papyrus parchment with pithy trails
its treasures stolen long ago
Her eyes were wet coal
 just placed upon the fire
Smoke curling round its edges
Her lipstick leaked like a crushed poppy
over her dentures
Her cough carried a barrowful of phlegm
that could not be emptied
Her hands wavered as she drew
another cigarette to her mouth
Her age spots like two day old porridge
left in a bowl
I tasted her presence
long after she had returned home

Johnny the Bull

The Vagaries of Grace

Being a fairweather cyclist
I pushed headlong into the delicious breeze
Sun sweetened hayfields
Delighting in the ease of the day
Like being hit by a benign light

I stopped by Johnny the Bull
Gargantuan in his magnificent seat
He looked at me with mild disinterest
I held in my bag some photographs
for the old bachelor who called him
His Big Pet

My unease founded in news
that his owner had died
He would never see the photograph
grace his mantlepiece
I was left with this gift
that meant little to anyone else
It wrapped me in a desperation
that deepened the day Johnny
vanished from the field

It's a lonely spot on the road now
I can't help but smile
When I think of the old man
clapping his rough hands and
cackling at his own jokes
standing by the gate

The Sum of all Things

Sun spoke to her lengthening shadows
Beckoned along coastal paths
of green golden grasses
Warmth on their blades
an absence of most day winds
brought scaled back silence
one could hear her estuary breath
the beating heart upon which we tread
Harvest moon pulled her peachy skirts
to full height
and bay basked in her sweetness
Evensong birds arrived
to taste her nectar
and bathe in her honeyed light
She cools to her bright brilliance
as she soars heavenward
Each pebble blade and grain
taking on sharp contrast
Slowly softening my early morning pain

Thunderstorm

Aine stood up from the sewing machine. Her back ached. She went over to the range and put the kettle on to boil on the hot plate. Taking out a scone she had baked earlier, it was still warm, and the butter softly melted down the side. She placed the tea leaves in the teapot with the scalding water, leaving it to draw for a few minutes before pouring out a hot steaming mug of comfort, a little milk and some sugar. She wrapped her thin hands around the warmth as it softened the discomfort in her fingers.

She warmed her bony hips against the range; not really tasting the scone. She swallowed hard and washed it down with the tea. Looking around the tiny parlour, baby Joseph in his cot, his eyes rolling deep in sleep. The remains of the washing hanging over the range were almost dry. She managed to get it in with the first puttering of rain on the window sill.

Rain now rapped its icy knuckles against the panes. The wind started to beat itself mercilessly, growling around outside like a Banshee desperate to gain entry to the cottage. Aine drew her cardigan tightly across her chest as the barn door started banging. She will get drenched. She considered running across the inky black yard; the constancy of the noise was tormenting her.

Billy should have been home hours ago from his fishing trip. The rising anxiety lodged in her throat as the clock ticked idly by, unaware of the anxiety that swam around its rhythm. She lifted the latch and pushed against the blunt snarl of the wind and into the yard. The icy rain spat furiously like stinging arrows. It took all of her strength to close the barn door. She stood breathlessly with her back against it and stared blindingly out into the black sea.

Billy, a softly spoken man who was economical with his words. The big ocean skies suited him. He was happiest working alone on his boat. However, the rhythms of nature spared no one's sentiments. Neighbouring island women held their own silent vigils behind closed doors.

Aine made her way back across the screaming yard. The turbulence buffeting her from behind and almost lifting her off her feet. Back in the sanctuary of the warm kitchen, she took off her dripping clothes in front of the fire and dried herself. Glancing over at her son, she said a silent prayer of thanks that he continued to sleep on through the storm.

She lifted her bony frame from the chair and got her beads from the bedside table. Sitting in front of the burning embers, she focused on the movement of the flames as she quietly recited the rosary. The gentle, rhythmic rise and fall of her infant's chest in sweet oblivion steadied her as she prayed, fingers earnestly pressing on the beads. Exhaustion overtook her, and in the steel grey light before dawn, a cry sprung from her throat as she saw a light from a lamp pierce the gloaming. Some of her male neighbours were carrying Billy between them. Her fortitude crumbled as she made for the small procession.

"Billy..." Her whole world had been gently woven around him from the first day she laid eyes on him.

The men laid his body on their marriage bed and set about preparing him. Words of unspeakable sorrow lodged in her throat, lamenting all of her tomorrows. Aine lifted her son to her breast and rocked him comfortlessly into the grey dawning.

Time Capsule

"Go on, try it". Sarah bit down hard on the green apple from the garden. The powerful bitterness pooled acid-like on the inside of her cheeks, immediately bringing a painful sensation to her back teeth. Even if she spat the vile bitterness into her hand, she could only place it in her pocket. Rather than do that, she swallowed. It brought water to her sixteen-year-old eyes, the acid already attacking her tooth enamel. "I don't think they are ripe enough yet".

Nelly was 79 and mostly bedbound. Sarah had visited the elderly in the nursing home and agreed to call on Nelly when she was sent home. Sarah knocked and waited. The bird-like creature greeted her "Go on in there.." Nelly made her way into the room and closed the door, struggling with the heavy blankets that had been nailed over the door frame.

 She returned to the bed that consumed most of the room. A small fire was lighting. The curtains were drawn shut, retracting the glorious sunshine. Fetid smells filled the oxygen-deprived room. Nelly rummaged through the detritus on the bed.

Picking up a tiny metal box and opening it, she pinched the brown powder, raised it to her nostrils and snorted on top of an old stain.

"Haven't you ever seen snuff..?", wiping her nose with the dirty handkerchief.

"It's great to clear your head."

"My womb started to fall out, you see, and the doctor said I need to spend lots of time in bed." Tall stacks of newspapers sat in unsteady piles on worn lino burnt by old hot coals. Sarah felt dizzy.

"Will you recite the Rosary with me?"

Nelly spoke of the day she went to mass with her mother during the civil war when gunmen came down from the hill and shot men in front of them in the street.

"Could you make me some tea before you go? There is some meat outside."

Sarah fought her way into the tiny hallway. Cold claws reached out to her from the damp walls. There was a steep, narrow stairwell next to the tiny scullery.

"Don't go upstairs!" Nelly called out. Sarah had no intention of going anywhere near upstairs. She struck a match and lit the gas to boil the kettle. Inhaling the sulphur, she placed a spoon of tea leaves into the teapot, leaving it to stand for a moment. The milk on the sideboard had condensation running down the icy glass.

Sarah fumbled with the latch, handing over the tea, "I couldn't see any meat."

"It's there, check the bottom step of the stairs."

Sarah had missed the tiny utilitarian stainless steel bowl on the step. There was a small lump of indeterminable meat lying in the greasy bowl.

"Is this what you want?" handing her the bowl.

"Yes, thank you."

"You have saved me a trip out of the bed."

"How do you get upstairs to the bathroom?"

"Oh, I haven't been up there in years, I have a pot under the bed."

Sarah thought about the pot's contents.

"I must be going now, do you need anything else?"

"No dear, thank you, just call again won't you?"

"Can you make sure that you close the door properly on your way out?"

Sarah stood for a moment in the hot sunny street recalibrating her senses. Sweet-smelling fresh air filled her lungs. Why had she felt being so frightened in this tiny woman's world? Was she going to end her days like this too? She looked at her young stong legs and said a silent prayer of thanks.

Velcro Dreams

My earliest regret in admitting I had some ability was when I turned three and eleven months. It was early Summer, and like many children my age, we started school a few months before the Summer holidays, to get settled in.

The young Presentation nun asked one day with her biggest smile
"Who can tie shoelaces?"
I had started out early in my career in the pursuit of other people's happiness.
My little hand shot up, calling out "I can, Sister!"

The pride of being the *Only One* quickly lost its gloss as I knelt on
the unforgiving marble floor of the Junior Infant's cloakroom. Starting from
the corner, the low bench ran the length of the space. Little hooks overhead
clasping tiny coats, and beneath, the bench housed a multitude of pigeon holes.
Nestled within each one, a small pair of leather lace-up shoes, or t-bar sandals with
the buckle to the side.

I looked in dismay at the long line of little knees and expectant shoes impatient to house the all-important feet before running out into the yard to play. The squeals of games being played taunting my fumbling fingers through the high window over our young heads. The line of tapping brown shoes looked like the Great Wall of China that I had seen in Encyclopaedia Britannica. My mother paid for it weekly to the man who called to the door. It was going to take forever to traverse.

I sighed and quietly cursed my enthusiasm. This became my daily ritual for the next two months. All of the "maith an cailín's" and gold stars in my copybook never made up for time lost playing in the schoolyard.

Visiting Molly Keane's Grave

The gate looked with idle curiosity
as I pushed against it
the metal under my hands
Biting my lip
the copper taste floods my mouth
Snarling winds slice headstones
Glancing off buttresses
red poppies
staggered drunkenly
Beacons
of blood, shit, deep deep rest
Babe placed on breast
Chords cut, but never fully
Quill carved on headstone
Black ravens beating in my chest
Flying from my throat
and piercing your heart
with their beaks
It splits open
hot frothy blood released
Not long enough to love you
And far too long for me

Voltage

Stepping into the psychiatric unit
my sister and I, filled with dread
Conspicuous in our school uniforms
to visit our mother
If they ask, say you are twelve
was all our father said

The air had a glue like quality
A stuckness of mind, soul and body
overlaid with a clawing warmth
A desperate air wrapped in
chemical stultification

We passed patients
shuffling in slippered feet
Our eyes placed firmly upon
the marble floor
the dread of catching what they had
consumed us

The sight of mother
the white crispness of the bed linen
Her glorious red hair framing her sleeping face
Drool pooling from her bottom lip
onto the pristine sheet

All we could see was her head
in that giant bed
With eyes closed
She spoke in a language
no one understood

What lands did our mother now walk in?
Would she ever return?
Why had he taken us there?
Had we badgered him to the point
of giving in to quieten us?

He had to slake his thirst
My sister and I walked the short walk
through the fields in miserable silence
Too afraid to utter the words
Will she ever come home

Waiting Room

There were days
that you hardly moved from the chair
bought on Hire Purchase
Costing you the fortune
you didn't have

Tiny slippered feet turned in at the toes
A small indicator of the gradual
turning inward taking place

Everything you wore
sat loosely upon your shrinking
Skirts too long, jumpers too wide
A mishmash of mis-matched
second hand items
Someone thought
about you to call
and give you something
That it didn't fit, didn't matter

You sat with your hands on your lap
Open palms on top of each other
As if waiting for that invisible host
to be placed there
Your faith had kept you going

The quiet remoteness
drew a veil across your eyes
as the fire reflected in them
on summer days
Long swatches of time
spent in that place of
just waiting

How reduced you have become
This tiny house
a testimony to your reduction
from the vibrant madness
of a household of ten
Adapting, forever adapting
to new untenable situations
that knocked the stuffing
the very life from you
and wore you down
to a place you resigned
not to get up from

Please walk with me in the garden
The south facing space
in a blaze of light
With slow reluctance
you took my arm
and walked into the sunshine

From that place
you point out
the landmarks that
shaped your existence

The church where you married
The hospital in which
you birthed your eight
and held them to your breast
And where you would die
The home you reared us in
the first two decades of marriage
All laid out from your garden
Like pages turning in
your storybook, though
the story no longer held your interest

Your modest domestic situation
and simple trinkets
belie the complexity of your nature
and the depths of your fractured soul

Your thoughts turn again inwards
to your son who left before you
You went with him that day
For what remained contained little
as you sat and waited
for your moment in patient prayer

God heard your fervent murmurs
that fateful night when you fell
to the hospital floor
Relief was granted you with
the sleep you did not wake from

Rest easy now dearest mother

My Somewhere in a Small Town

Mr O'Brien's filthy car is abandoned outside Dunphy's pub. The windows are open, and the sheepdog bares his teeth as I pass by. Nelly is across the road tapping the last drop of petrol into the Ford Escort then screws the cap on. The Main Guard clock chimes twelve noon not quite in sync with the church up the street. Two harried mothers brush past. Their prams bouncing weeping babies and groceries. Toddlers refusing to keep pace, their small arms overstretched on the handles. The Sacred Heart medals held firmly in place with nappy pins and prayers.

Mrs Dunphy has run the small grocery shop with the snug bar for as long as I can remember. She has an adult daughter, but I have never seen her husband. She has large grimy hands and sweaty breasts. Her body odour follows her around. Her short brown hair is nipped off her forehead with a hair clip. She licks the nib of the pencil to write up the tab in her copybook.

"That's two large loaves, a bottle of milk, and a head of cabbage".
"Tell your mother I'll have the yeast in tomorrow".

Glancing at the opaque glass in the swing doors, I could make out two figures inside. The desire to push my hands on the glass and poke my head inside almost took me over.

No self-respecting woman would be seen going in there apart from Mrs Dunphy. She has a way of licking her thumb and reverentially rolling the squashed notes thrown on the counter by old men in wellingtons that smell of cowshit. She also has a way of touching her temple and brushing an imaginary hair from her flushed cheek when Matty Bergin comes in. He hands her his wife's grocery list, orders a large bottle and steps inside the fulcrum. I take quiet pleasure from her fluttering discomfiture.

Stepping back, I glance my ankle on the crates stacked with empties. The delivery man is loading them on the back of the lorry. The sound of the chiming glass sends a ripple of pleasure through me.

"Are you alright dear?" Mrs Dunphy enquires pulling close the open button in the middle of her bosom with one hand. She wore the same crimpline blouse and brown tweed skirt all year round. She must wash them and let them drip dry overnight.

"I'll be with you as soon as I pour Mr Bergin his pint".

She glances at her reflection, putting on a sly slick of orange lipstick on the fissured broken flesh of her lips in the Smithwicks mirror. She stared at me with a thickened gaze, and I look down at my shoes.

Where Does Winter Go

The icy splinters from the muck puddle clings to your boot
Its watery membrane, a memory
The grass snaps under your feet
tiny twigs releasing their frosty coats in your wake
The trees in the lane cast you doubtful glances
as hail stones ring on their naked branches
Impaling the slick leafy carpet, your head and shoulders

The gloomy light greets you
Its slow reluctance to depart
Billowing chimneys fill your nostrils
Their tarry tendrils grasp and fill your hair
Blackbird already soundly sleeping
as you raise your shoulders against watery winds
and turn homebound

Winter Walk

On the eve of Christmas Eve
the November dead laid to rest
and candles blessed
The day carried a softness to it
A mildness of light
and estuary enjoyed a
sparse sprinkling of early Gorse
The scent of honeysuckle
in fragrant folds
on the sea breeze
Its sweetness, a promise
of tomorrow's Springs
the Cock's step unfolding
to brighter days ahead

Rooks from the Lookout

Setting their elemental clocks
They drape their blue black wings
over sleepy heads
Waking Eastern skies blush
as the Celestial Army rises
from its somewhere place

With halting chorus
their incandescence flits
with each rising breath
morning sun takes
a slow heave upon the horizon

On and on Battalions come
A never ending procession
Or so it seems
Above milky morning waves
A chordal congruence
Just as they arrive
They are gone
Leaving a fleeting gift
Of Wonder

About the Author

Martine O'Donovan hails from Clonmel, County Tipperary and grew up with the smell of Bulmers apples in her hair. Writer and Artist, Martine has been writing and painting for many years. She lives by the sea in Tramore, County Waterford with her family. Its elemental beauty, her history, family and friends are a constant source of inspiration. This is her first book of poetry and short stories. She is currently working on her first novel.

Photo credit thanks to Malgorzata Piech.

Please Review

Dear Reader,

If you enjoyed this book, would you kindly post a short review on whichever platform you purchased from? Your feedback will make all the difference to getting the word out about this book.

Thank you in advance.

Lough Mohra, Rathgormack, County Waterford

Lightning Source UK Ltd.
Milton Keynes UK
UKHW020949071220
374691UK00003B/86